EARTH!

My First 4.54 Billion Years

For Frank, my brother and fellow Earthling —S. M.

For Katie, Ben, and George —D. L.

For all my humans, especially the ones who recycle! —E.

ISBN 978-1-338-59930-5

Published by Scholastic Inc., 557 Broadway, New York, NY 10012, by arrangement with Henry Holt and Company.

12 11 10 9 8 7 6 5 4 3 2 1 19 20 21 22 23 24

Printed in the U.S.A. 76

This edition first printing, September 2019

Designed by April Ward

The illustrations for this book were created with pencils, ink, watercolor paints, and digital art tools.

EARTH!

MY FIRST 4.54 BILLION YEARS

BY Earth (WITH STACY MCANULTY)

ILLUSTRATED BY Earth (AND DAVID LITCHFIELD)

SCHOLASTIC INC.

Hi! My name is
Earth.
Some people call me
Gaia,
the blue
marble,

the
WORLD,
or the third planet from the sun.
You can call me
Planet Awesome.

My family is
really, really big.

I have seven siblings in my solar system.
I'm closest to Venus and Mars.
Some used to say I have eight siblings,
but Pluto is more like the family pet.

And then there are my cousins.
My Milky Way family has billions of planets.
Told you. **BIG** family.

My favorite things to do are spinning—
it takes me a whole day to go around once—

and CIRCLING the SUN.

That takes me an entire year.

My best friend is the moon. We hang out all the time, even when you can't see her. The moon needs 27 days, 7 hours, 43 minutes, and 12 seconds to go around me. I've timed her.

7 HRS
43:12

I was born 4.54 billion years ago.

I don't remember what it was like to be a baby. Who does? But I've been told I was a hot mess.

Explosive. Gassy! Very cranky.

Then I started to cool off, and things got wet.
Really wet.
It rained for thousands of years.
(I'm not kidding: thousands!)

I was soggy and lonely. A few islands popped up in my oceans, but no plants or animals.

My islands must have been lonely, too. They got together and made bigger islands called continents.

I remember Ur and Nuna and the ginormous Pangea.

Then Pangea split into seven separate continents.

Things are always changing.

As I got older, stuff began to grow.

LIFE!

400,000,000
years ago
And then come bugs.

2,400,000,000
years ago
Air! If anyone had been alive, they could finally take a breath!

470,000,000 years ago
Plants that can live on land.

(ALMOST HALF MY LIFE)
You probably wouldn't even recognize me! (Though I've always been round.)

4,540,000,000
years ago
I arrive!

150,000,000 years ago
Birds. Did you know they are relatives of dinosaurs?
Hi
200,000 years ago
Homo sapiens! You humans have big brains and walk on two feet.
130,000,000 years ago
Flowers. I'm a very pretty planet. It's not bragging if it's true.
210,000,000 years ago
Yay for mammals! They're fuzzy and warm.
240,000,000 years ago
My first dinosaur!
NOW

The time of the dinosaurs was one of my favorites.

I mean, everyone loves dinosaurs!
They lived with me for 175 million years.

UntiL . . .

ASTEROID!!

It's not always
easy being Earth.
Volcanic
eruptions.